WINNING WAYS

*A Guide to Succeed
in Business, Sales and Life*

DANIEL HOLTE

Copyright © 2014 F&D Creations, LLC

WINNING WAYS: A Guide to Succeed in Business, Sales and Life

All rights reserved. No part of this publication may be reproduced, distributed, or transmitted in any form or by any means, including photocopying, recording, or other electronic or mechanical methods, without the prior written permission of the author, except in the case of brief quotations embodied in critical reviews and certain other noncommercial uses permitted by copyright law. For permission requests, email the author, addressed "Attention: Permissions Coordinator," at the email address below:

Email: danielholtewinningways@gmail.com

Website: www.winningwaysbook.com

Printed in the United States of America

First Printing, 2012

ISBN-13: 978-1502906168

ISBN-10: 1502906163

Co-author: Darla Swanson

©2014 F&D Creations, LLC | *WINNING WAYS: A Guide to Succeed in Business, Sales and Life* | All Rights Reserved | No reproduction permitted without approval from F&D Creations, LLC

CONTENTS

BUSINESS PHILOSOPHY 1

FOREWORD 2

INTRODUCTION 3

CHAPTER 1: FIVE STEPS OF SELLING 11
  FIVE BASIC STEPS OF SELLING
  ELEMENTS OF A GOOD PROPOSAL
  QUICK REFERENCE – CHAPTER 1

CHAPTER 2: OVERCOMING OBJECTIONS 25
  OVERCOMING YOUR PROSPECT'S OBJECTIONS
  WORKING A BOOTH
  QUICK REFERENCE – CHAPTER 2

CHAPTER 3: EDUCATION 33
  WHY GET AN EDUCATION?
  SELF-EDUCATION TOOLS
  QUICK REFERENCE – CHAPTER 3

CHAPTER 4: SELF-DISCIPLINE 41
  FIVE BENEFICIAL AREAS OF SELF-DISCIPLINE
  QUICK REFERENCE – CHAPTER 4

CHAPTER 5: TEAMWORK 49
  SEVEN ELEMENTS OF A TEAM ATTITUDE
  MENTORING LESSONS
  QUICK REFERENCE – CHAPTER 5

CHAPTER 6: DOCUMENTATION 59
  THREE BASIC AREAS OF DOCUMENTATION
  IF FILES ARE A MESS
  QUICK REFERENCE – CHAPTER 6

A FINAL NOTE 67

BUSINESS PHILOSOPHY

There are two things in the business world that are vitally important to remember: Nothing happens until the sale is made and we are each a salesperson. It doesn't matter if you are in sales or are an executive secretary, a store clerk or a bank teller. We are all selling the company, organization or industry we represent.

In this book we will take a look at the basic skills needed to succeed in business (specifically sales), including: core principles of sales, honesty, loyalty, promptness, organization, studiousness, knowing yourself, communication skills and much more.

Foreword

I was invited to join NCR by one of the company's most vocal supporters, Daniel Holte. It wasn't just a job — I was welcomed into the NCR family. This man also welcomed me into his own family. Who is this guy, Daniel Holte?

Daniel is a believer in people, a promoter of people, who takes pride in his track record of hiring people who did their job well and continued to move up the corporate and social ladder. Daniel has a gift, a knack, for bringing people along. He does this by working side by side with them. He preached to us about the "how's" and the "why's," but not from a lofty position — from a roll up the sleeves, eyeball to eyeball next to you in order to get the job done kind of way.

Dan taught me the "Bell Cow Theory." A herd of cattle only has one bell cow, the leader — the one the other cows follow. Within the business world successful people can be an incentive to others in a group, and Daniel was like that.

I adopted many of the lessons I learned from Daniel while he was at NCR. When he left, I was offered the district manager position he vacated. I managed sales districts for the next 13 years. I was a successful district manager due in large part to my NCR upbringing, influenced heavily by Daniel Holte. There are many other people that he influenced in the same manner.

Working with and for Daniel was the catalyst for a friendship that has proven to have lifelong staying power. There is no one else that even comes close to having provided so much opportunity and reward to me in both my professional and my personal life. If you know Daniel Holte, you are a blessed person.

Thanks, Dan. You're the best!

Steve Reinke ~ NCR/Teradata Corporation
Partnership Marketing, Retired

INTRODUCTION

"Everyone lives by selling something." ~Robert Louis Stevenson

      This book was inspired by a request from my young nephew, Pete, who graduated from the Air Force Academy, completed six years of active duty and resigned Captain. He was about to enter civilian life and begin a new line of work, chasing his dreams. I was recently retired, looking forward to fun and relaxation, hunting, fishing and gardening.

      What follows flows out of my correspondence with Pete, taken from a series of letters we exchanged. Outlined in the chapters of this book are more formal explanations of the disciplines and methods that helped me succeed beyond my wildest dreams — proven methods for winning at sales.

* * * * * * * * * * * * * * * * * *

Dear Pete:

I am flattered that you have asked me to help you as your mentor. My style is old-fashioned and sometimes difficult for your generation to accept. You probably won't find my methods outlined in any MBA program, but they work.

You have shared with me a factor in your life that I am quite familiar with, namely money problems. I discovered early on that the only help for money problems would come from myself or be divine. Not even my parents would or could help. Resist filing bankruptcy because it will follow you even into your business life. When I was young and had money problems, I resisted bankruptcy and worked my way out of the problem by honestly explaining my situation to creditors and offering a repayment plan we both could live with. I'd like to share some points that helped me and will help you as well.

#1: Learn to manage your finances.

If you can't manage your personal financial affairs how could you possibly hope to manage any business financially — be it your own or someone else's?

#2: Stick with what you are good at.

I have always stuck with familiar endeavors. The one time I violated this rule I lost my butt. I had a great idea, but since I didn't completely understand the industry, it failed. When you find something you enjoy and understand, stick with it! I spent 40 years selling equipment to commercial banks. I stuck with this philosophy both in my own business and when I worked for others. When you stick with something long enough you become an expert and are recognized by the business community you serve.

#3: Do not put your family at risk.

You are young and can afford to wait before you go into business for yourself. Rome wasn't built in a day, and fame or fortune can't be either. There is no magic formula, but hard work over extended time. If your present job provides adequate income, opportunity and growth potential, stay with it. Your time will come when either you will be promoted or can start your own business. I worked for NCR over 19 years and had my ups and downs, but finally was able to leave for greener pastures.

#4: Find someone who is successful and follow them.

Your boss, or someone else in your company, can help you learn and advance faster than you can accomplish by yourself. Don't befriend the sea lawyers or losers — they will only drag you down with them. Be discerning, stand back and evaluate both your supervisor and peer group and develop business relationships with the winners.

#5: Limit your business relationships in your personal social life.

Be kind, helpful and willing to help your co-workers and supervisors, but do not make the mistake of getting too comfortable socially. Business and social life don't mix well and sooner or later one will be compromised.

#6: Start on the road to financial success by discipline.

A good formula is to give 10% to God, save 10% and spend 80%. Start now! Don't wait — it's already too late! Pay God first and he will help you achieve your goal of financial independence. When my wife, Darlene, convinced me to live up to my responsibility to God she agreed to do her part by managing the balance of our income conservatively. It took time but gradually our financial problems disappeared. Pay yourself next by saving. Don't wait until all of your bills are paid. Start to save on a disciplined basis now. Save long-term and resist any temptation to take your savings and spend it. When you earn a commission or get a raise, take the after-tax balance, save half and spend the rest. Have some fun, you've earned it!

When you finally buy a home, begin with the first payment to apply extra money against the principal. Pay this extra amount on a monthly basis and your home will be paid off sooner than you think. A home without a mortgage is a valuable asset. If you own your own home, you only have to feed yourself and not worry about a roof over your head.

#7: When you start a business do not invest any more money in the business than necessary.

We started BANKSYSTEMS with a capital investment of $2,000. During the 20 years I was CEO we did not recapitalize even though we grew to some $15 million a year in sales. How was this possible? Our contracts required a 50% down payment. This down payment was unprecedented for most vendors selling to commercial banks, but we were never turned down and our success ratio was very high.

The effectiveness of our proposal, user list and contract inclusion worked like magic. Since we did business on a national scale it wasn't always possible to visit each prospect. Our sales were mostly made by phone contact, plus a very effective proposal. We were able to train inexperienced salespeople to close business quickly and effectively via the phone and mail. This method saved money and allowed us to create new business with a small amount of starting capital. We also used only a small amount of operating capital with 4% of our expenses paid through a line of credit.

You do the math. If you anticipated $15 million in sales and required capital to fund business that turned over in approximately 60 days, your line of credit for the year would be approximately $500,000. The secret: A down payment of 50% and a historical 42% gross operating expense.

Our success illustrates that the right sales plan and asking for a down payment can work. This method was time-tested and provided many advantages:

1. Reduced capital requirements.

2. Eliminated the temptation for the customer to cancel the contract.

3. Built growth without the use of our own capital.

4. Eliminated the need for outside investors.

NOTE: Work, whenever possible, with other people's money.

#8: Resist the temptation to include family in any business ventures. Also, resist the temptation to include an active partner.

I made these mistakes and you can learn from me. A partner, even a minority partner, can cause many problems. Most of the problems created by a partner won't raise their ugly heads until you get down the road, and then they are impossible to correct. A minority partner could become your worst nightmare, a competitor and a minority stockholder all at the same time.

IN SHORT:

1. Correct your financial situation. It's a distraction.

2. Stick with the familiar.

3. Do not put your family at risk.

4. Associate with successful people.

5. Business and social life don't mix.

6. Organize a financial formula for your life.

7. Do not invest any more money in a business than necessary.

8. No family or partners in any future business.

There are many more specifics that we can talk about. Digest this, critique the information and write again.

Love, Uncle Dan

* * * * * * * * * * * * * * * * * * * *

Dear Pete:

I have been spending many hours each evening in my bear stand. No luck so far, but the bear gets regular meals for free since he visits when I am not in my stand. The many solitary hours spent in the woods gives me a chance to think about my commitment to help mentor you.

The other night my thoughts turned to the many young people I trained during my work life. Some of them followed my advice and succeeded and some did not. All of these young men and women were well educated (BA/BS minimum, MBA's, CPA's, etc.), but all were members of the baby boom generation. I will not attempt to explain their many inadequacies, but generally, they lacked motivation and creativity and were not self-starters. They were used to having someone else do the difficult tasks for them and they were lazy. They generally thought they deserved success since they were well-educated. They were all, however, smart, good looking and willing to be paid large sums of money for little productivity.

A quote that comes to mind by football legend Lou Holtz is, "Your talent determines what you can do. Your motivation determines how much you are willing to do. Your attitude determines how well you do it."

Success will follow those people who apply themselves to the basics and become students of their chosen profession. Life or a career are not 8:00 a.m. to 5:00 p.m. jobs, but a daily application of good habits, honesty, study and self-starting motivation. Vince Lombardi, General Curtis LeMay, Billy Graham and many others taught us to begin with the basics. Lombardi with football, LeMay with a new branch of the Armed Forces and Billy Graham who taught the basics of salvation. They all are considered great men, at the very top of their professions.

Love, Uncle Dan

Dear Uncle Dan:

Good morning! It's 6:11 a.m., and I'm at work. I've followed your advice (on coming early and staying late) for one full week. It's not that I didn't do that before, I just never committed to it as a measure of my willingness to the commitment required for success.

I was excited to get your letters and I've put them in a binder, highlighted important ideas, plus I'm using those ideas to create a weekly check sheet to measure myself on. One thing I have learned is the value of truthful self-measurement in any undertaking.

I've also been adding my notes, tasks and schedule from each day, which I reviewed for lessons learned this weekend — very valuable, and a discipline that I'll continue. Your advice on business writing was well taken. I'm eagerly waiting for the next installment of "Holte Success 101" and am curious what the topics will be….

Love, Pete

Chapter 1

Five Steps of Selling

"Always be closing… That doesn't mean you're always closing the deal, but it does mean that you need to be always closing on the next step in the process." ~Shane Gibson

All good businesspeople are salespeople, even those who are not in direct sales. There are many different selling environments or jobs. A sales job in retail involves different methods than, say, a highly technical one selling computers and software.

Great salespeople are good communicators and good at providing understandable solutions for problems. For those of us who are not naturally great at these skills, the elements needed to become great are attainable through hard work.

This chapter explains a structured approach to selling. There are formal sales jobs and less formal sales jobs. Since this structured approach is most applicable to highly technical products (a formal sales job), certain elements, like a written proposal, can be disregarded when it comes to less formal or technical sales (retail or auto).

The structured approach used in formal sales jobs, such as selling computer systems to banks or other businesses, is found in:

Five Basic Steps of Selling

1. The Approach
2. The Survey
3. The Proposal
4. The Demonstration
5. The Close

A less formal sales job (like retail or car sales) can use the same approach, but it will look a little different.

Suppose you are selling shoes for a retail store. In a formal sales job you perform the approach, but in shoe sales, your prospect helps in the approach by visiting your store looking to purchase shoes. Your sales job will be to survey their needs, finding out what style, color, size and use is desired.

Note that knowledge of your store's inventory will help you satisfy the customer purchase. The knowledge gained during the survey (determining size, color, style, etc.), put together with your understanding of the store's inventory, will help you satisfy the prospect's needs and make your sale. You both achieve satisfaction — the customer gets new shoes and you get a commission.

Suppose you aren't selling a pair of shoes to an individual, but are selling a manufacturer's line of shoes to major retailers. Your methods will change to a more formal method that includes a written proposal (less formal will be a verbal proposal). Your product line of shoes will dictate some of the proposal's content. Selling high fashion shoes vs. hunting footwear requires different information. High fashion won't require protective toes, temperature or moisture protection. Your proposal must appropriately highlight the important selling features of your product.

A successful salesperson concentrates his proposal on only the important features or values of their product. Take the time to understand your competition's product differences and strengths. Then concentrate your proposal on the advantages of your system, with emphasis on those features that counter your competitors. Do not, however, mention in the proposal your competitor's name, product features or any advantage they might possess. Concentrate on selling your product's values and advantage.

If you do a good job writing and presenting your proposal, your prospect will make the proper choice. A little salesperson trick of comparison can help. If your product includes exclusive features or values, highlight them. This will give you an advantage and maybe put your competition on the defense.

Let's take a closer look at the five basic steps in selling to gain a more complete understanding of what they entail. The definitions that follow fit in with a more formal sales job, but can be altered for a less formal sales job.

1. The Approach

Initial contact should, if possible, be completed in person. I am fully aware that telemarketing is popular and effective; however, this method should be confined to certain situations and by well-seasoned salespersons. If you want to set up a meeting with a possible prospect consider calling the secretary and asking for a scheduled visit whenever the boss is available. Introduce yourself, the company you represent and why you want to meet. Ask the secretary to help you, since you have important information for the boss. Use your imagination — your goal is a face-to-face meeting.

The approach will determine if you will be allowed to continue on with the selling process or have the door shut on you. First impressions are important and it is vital that you appeal to your prospect on his or her turf. Always be willing to discuss any general or personal interest that might be brought up by the prospect during the approach. For a "newbie" salesperson, you will grow with experience and should become proficient in this important skill.

Other than in rare instances, you will always have competition, sometimes even from within the company you work for. If you possess a diverse knowledge, including familiarity with your prospect's business, your contribution to the conversation will help you develop a natural bond. Talking about subjects that interest your prospect by making observations (notice the pictures on the wall or interesting artifacts and personal touches in the office) and by asking questions will help your prospect be more receptive to you.

2. The Survey

The survey is a process of gathering information. A survey might be formal or casual. It is usually conducted by working with people that produce the day-to-day activity your proposal will focus on. This might mean that your initial contact would be a manager or corporate officer responsible for the division or department you have targeted, or maybe the president. Obviously the president of a corporation isn't going to help you with all the necessary details, so ask him who you should work with. Ask your contact if they would mind introducing you to the people you are making the survey with. An introduction from your contact to the people involved is powerful and will establish the importance of your survey.

By the way, sell your contact on the benefits of your survey, and that you plan to prepare a proposal (step three) on your findings. Remember that during the actual survey you are on a fact-finding mission, with a goal of applying your idea(s) or product. Take notes! Keep the notes as a learning resource, to be reviewed the next time you are involved in a similar situation.

When doing the survey, get to know the staff. If possible, include them in your written proposal, and take a few words to thank them. It is important to have the staff on your side, even if they are not a part of the decision making process for the company. Tell them you are completing the survey in the hope that you will be able to help both them and their company. The survey is another opportunity to test your ideas and sell them to the staff that ultimately will use your product or idea.

3. The Proposal

A proposal is a formal document that is useful in selling a product or program to an audience. Correctly prepared, it will help you sell to others within your target audience who you can't reach personally. In other words, you might be making the presentation of your proposal to a vice president, but he in turn will share the proposal with the final decision maker — the board of directors or the president of the company. Since you might not be able to present to final decision makers in person, your proposal will do the job for you, so write your proposal accordingly.

A proposal is an important piece of communication in the selling process. Good communication in any form (verbal or written) means the ability to make your point with the fewest words. Wordy presentations are boring. Get to the point and go on from there. After the main presentation, go back and summarize important information.

Concentrate on the meat. Perhaps you remember the famous ad campaign for the fast food chain, Wendy's. While looking at a fictional competitor's burger, an actress asked, "Where's the beef?" The point was well-taken and people remembered the message. Don't be tempted to add filler to your message. Save your thank you for the close (step five). If your audience won't read past the first sentence or paragraph, they should not be thanked.

Since your first sentence or paragraph might be the last chance you have to capture your audience's attention, do not waste this golden opportunity on filler or salutations.

Limit your sales points to no more than five. Take some time to rank your sales points according to what you think will be the most important to your audience, since you are selling *to them* and not yourself. Once you rank your sales points, go back and explain each one of them. Explain the most important feature of each point first, followed by the next most important. Stop once you adequately explain each point — before you become redundant.

Your proposal should be presented verbally, and not read. A verbal presentation of the proposal separates the winners from the losers. It's somewhat of a gift but even those of us who aren't gifted in this way can do a creditable job if we prepare. Hand your prospect his copy and then begin to present the proposal contents from memory. It is always helpful to write your presentation down.

Computer- or video-aided presentation:

Your screen will provide a visual aide for your presentation. The screen should summarize your sales points. The verbal presentation of these points must explain each sales point and their value for your prospect.

You must completely memorize each sales point and its value to effectively make your presentation verbatim. Practice, practice, practice! Be ready for interruptions and be familiar enough to restart your presentation once the interruption is satisfied. Good presenters understand their subject.

As you start with the most important and conclude with the least important, go back and represent the most important idea using different verbiage. This will reinforce the most important information in your proposal.

When practicing your presentation, read your written material over and over until it's committed to memory. Then, create a crib sheet on a 3x5 index card. Without referring to your original script, using only the card, attempt to re-write your presentation. If you can't re-write the presentation from the crib sheet, go back and study. Study until you can re-write from the card.

As part of your practice, go somewhere that you can verbally, out loud, make your presentation. Repeat this performance until you feel comfortable.

The day before your presentation do not attempt to study your script. Rest and relax. When you get up to make your presentation take a few moments and study your audience. Relax! You are in command.

Use the 3x5 index cards as a prompt only. Do not attempt to memorize your entire written script, but let the 3x5 cards be a guide as you in a relaxed manner, make your presentation. If you miss certain details (which only you will know) just keep going. You might even add the missing detail at the end of your presentation since no one will be the wiser.

Be yourself — don't read the script.

Study your material — relax, and have fun!

Make enough copies of your proposal for all that will attend your presentation. Ask during the approach or survey who will attend your presentation, or how many copies you might need. Make originals for each person since everyone wants to feel important. Again, consider the staff as a vital part of your sale. Everyone in the office should be treated like they are important because they are! For large company presentations expect there may include one, two or more individuals you do not know and their role(s) may not be identified. Remain calm and don't let them become a distraction to you.

NOTE: A written proposal on ideas or an internal corporate suggestion is also important since it establishes in writing the author and doesn't result in plagiarism.

I worked very hard during my career to produce the best-written proposals possible and I was very good at it. Some of my proposals were used by NCR Corporate to train young salespersons during formal Dayton schooling. I made an effort to produce excellent written proposals, customized for each situation. I kept copies of all my proposals and used them frequently as a resource for future situations.

Another key point is to retrieve all proposals that do not result in a positive sales result. Why? You don't want your ideas and style floating around for competitors to use against you by combating your ideas with their own. If you target a prospect that doesn't reward you with a positive decision, he doesn't deserve to keep your proposal. You might consider a diplomatic disclaimer somewhere in the writing in the proposal, which establishes your ownership.

ELEMENTS OF A GOOD PROPOSAL

A. Executive Summary or Overview

B. Systems Detail

C. Investment Analysis

D. Contracts (in case of a corporate idea this can be a formal sign-off sheet)

A. Executive Summary

The executive summary is a written document that is placed behind a tab in your proposal booklet. Yes, I said booklet, indexed by reference dividers. Your work should always be both neat and professional.

The executive summary should narrate in an easy-to-read form the most important details of your proposal. The executive summary is important since people other than your primary contact will be reading this section to get an overview. Remember to structure your executive summary starting with the most important element and proceeding to the least important. You want to captivate their attention with the first word or sentence in the hope they will read on to completion.

Don't be tempted to include any material or information in the executive summary that isn't important to the sale of your product or idea.

B. Systems Detail

Systems detail is a simple, organized document that defines your product or idea. Include advantages or special values in this document. Be specific and try not to use a template.

A template is usually produced on media dissimilar to the rest of your proposal. If you do use one, take some time and convert the template to the same media used for the entire proposal, including font type and size and any other formatting issues that may be inconsistent. This will make the proposal appear to be generated, completed and specifically formed for your prospect. Once the template is customized it can be successfully used in future proposals and make them all appear to be original.

C. Investment Analysis

An investment analysis is a breakdown of the individual costs of your proposal. It should include a breakdown of potential savings the proposed system will generate, and also include important values, such as improvements in schedules or accounts receivable collections, etc.

This section of your proposal can also be used to outline in writing both your own and your prospect's responsibilities, such as, "During the implementation of your system, training schedules will be established that are mutually acceptable."

You can also explain that a highly qualified trainer will be assigned as the implementation coordinator. For example: "We suggest that you (the customer) assign operating staff, along with their managers, for these sessions."

These written responsibilities will help avoid misunderstandings later.

D. Contracts

Always include completed contracts, or a sign-off sheet ready to be executed, in your proposal. Once you complete the presentation of your proposal attempt a trial close. A trial close is an attempt to seal the sale early in the selling process. This doesn't mean you don't have any more work to do, but if you have a signed contract the sale is made. After presenting the proposal you can say something like, "I have included these contracts (or, sign-off sheets) for your signature. As soon as you endorse them we can begin your project."

A trial close during the presentation of the proposal is simply an attempt to ask your prospect to buy. The trial close might be a response to their enthusiasm over certain features or ideas. Simply suggest that they sign so the values identified can begin. Listen to your prospect's response to your proposal, as they will send signals of acceptance during your presentations. Take advantage, and attempt to close the sale!

4. The Demonstration

This is difficult when selling a suggestion or idea, but a must for any equipment involved in your sale. Take the time to practice, practice, and practice! If you can't demonstrate effectively you will damage your efforts. With equipment, make sure you can handle anything your prospect asks. Make your demo look simple — you are supposed to be the expert! Demonstrate advantages and unique features. Highlight any advantage your competitor doesn't possess and without saying it directly, let your prospect know that you have something to offer that your competition doesn't. When I demonstrated to banks, I picked an application like the delinquent loan report and not payroll, since payroll was notoriously the easiest thing to demonstrate. I would subtly suggest that anyone can demo payroll, knowing that was my competitor's usual approach! When my competitor used payroll for his demo, my subtle suggestion worked like magic.

5. The Close

It doesn't matter how excellent your idea or how effective your solution is if you can't get the signature on the dotted line. You will fail. I have worked with salespeople most of my life that had a better education, were smarter and more accomplished, but they failed primarily because they could not close. I could!

Sometimes it's simply asking for the signature. You don't have to use tricks or trite methods. If you have done the first four steps properly, it's simple. Sign the contract or sign-off sheet. Remember, you will spend as much time preparing for a successful conclusion as you will for a failed one, so make each step count. Start out with a positive attitude and complete the basics of each step. Then, ask for the order.

Now you are on a roll! You have just closed the sale and are riding high! Don't be tempted to reward yourself by taking the afternoon off to play golf. Instead, reward yourself by attempting to close a sale that is in progress. The momentum and enthusiasm from the just-closed sale might help you complete another one. Just like football, your momentum can lead to another score!

A good salesperson has many sales projects in the works. When you complete a successful sale, review your sales that are in progress and attempt to conclude the most natural and obvious.

I traveled to a rural Electric Cooperative where my sales process was complete, except for the close. The sale was successfully closed with a contract signature and I left the building a happy salesperson, since the sale represented 2 ½ months of quota.

It had started to snow and I decided that since I was on a roll, I'd call another prospect and ask if I could meet with him that afternoon. The drive was difficult but upon arrival I demonstrated a new teller machine. My prospect purchased five new machines! Then, before I could leave, he inquired about a new proof machine we had just announced. He asked about the machine's feature, price and delivery. His enthusiasm suggested a trial close. Since delivery was many months away, I suggested he sign an order that very day.

He consulted with the bank president and decided to order two machines, as they anticipated growth. It was a sale of $40,000 – another two months quota for me. Wow! I sold five months' worth of business just because I was willing to use the momentum of my first success and keep working. I drove home some 80 miles in the snow, slipping and sliding – and smiling, a very happy salesman.

NOTE: Work on your storytelling skills! Stories are a great way to get a point across.

Another sales story comes to my mind about a woman who proved to be an expert in sales. Not just because she sold me her product, but because she was professional, and made no attempt to cut corners.

My wife and I finished raising our family in a suburb of Minneapolis. We began to make lots of money, and decided to purchase an old farm in northern Minnesota for a family retreat. We restored an old farmhouse, installed playgrounds, a pond, a swimming pool and developed a hunting paradise. Years went by and our large family grew to include six sons-in-law, two daughters-in-law and many grandchildren with more on the way. The farm also became a pleasant hunting retreat for the entire gang.

A number of personal events caused me to begin thinking of early retirement. My wife and I began to discuss moving to our hometown of Duluth, which was 45 miles north of the farm. One weekend while traveling to the farm, my wife asked me if I would like to retire at the farm. I enthusiastically endorsed her suggestion. She had one request and that was to build a new house. I told her to pick out the house and we built the new place on the site of the old farmhouse.

Our builder was an excellent contractor but lacked some of the finishing skills such as bathroom fixtures, kitchen design, etc. Our builder and plumber recommended that we visit a bathroom showroom in Duluth for advice. While there, we asked the salesperson if she knew anyone that had expertise in designing kitchens. She recommended a Duluth company, called the owner and set up a meeting for us that very afternoon. Upon arrival we were treated to a slide presentation by the owner. When she completed the slide presentation I told her we were ready to sign up for her service. "Not so fast," was her pleasant reply. First she wanted to make a survey, followed by a written proposal. The survey would include a series of questions about our cooking habits, cuisine, etc. The proposal would include three solutions based on the primary design of the kitchen. The three solutions were to provide a choice of different materials and cost solutions.

My first question was what her cost would be for the design and execution for the project. It was simple: $500 plus she would provide the material and appliances from our selection of one design. That's how she was compensated.

The survey was completed and included all the functions of a kitchen including what method would be used to cook various cuisines. Our home was going to be all electric but included availability of propane gas. As we discussed various appliances, oriental cooking came up. As I revealed that I liked to cook with a wok, we discussed that an electric stovetop wasn't good for oriental cooking. My wife and I also mentioned, however, that certain cooking methods did require an electric range. The saleswoman's solution was a counter top that includes both gas and electric burners.

Our contract included installation, which was sub-contracted. The installation and design was perfect and our choice of the most expensive proposal proved to be the most cost effective. Many refinements were provided beyond the proposal, making us happy customers.

Why do I believe that this woman was great at selling? She sold me — and that is not an easy task!

Quick Reference – Chapter 1

The five basic steps of selling:

➔ The Approach

➔ The Survey

➔ The Proposal, including:

> ➔ Executive Summary or Overview
>
> ➔ Systems Detail
>
> ➔ Investment Analysis
>
> ➔ Contracts

➔ The Demonstration

➔ The Close

Work on your storytelling skills!

Chapter 2

Overcoming Objections

"Obstacles don't have to stop you. If you run into a wall, don't turn around and give up. Figure out how to climb it, go through it or walk around it." ~Michael Jordan

Overcoming objections in selling often takes many forms. Sometimes objections are posed as questions and sometimes they are direct comments about your recommendations or features.

How you respond to an objection is very critical to your sale. How you answer the objection vs. your response to a simple question is also critical.

A question about your recommendation should be answered simply by stating the requested fact. An objection requires a more detailed response. You may need, for example, to give a detailed explanation of why a feature or fact will help your prospect.

Sometimes objections are prompted by your competitor and must be countered with the advantage or value of your proposal or recommendation. Knowledge of your competitor's strengths and weaknesses is helpful when addressing your prospect's objection. Win your prospect by:

1. Explaining the advantage of your system.

2. Understanding your prospect's needs and use this information to help them overcome their objection. A good survey will provide information that will help you.

3. Answering questions and objections with confidence and facts. Too many statements of "I don't know" or "I will do some research and get back to you" will destroy your credibility. Knowledge is key.

Once a certain bank cashier called me and requested the price of four proof and encoding machines. I asked him if I could study or survey his system requirements before I gave him a price. His objection was, "What could you possibly study or survey in my proof department that your system could improve?"

I initiated selling him on these facts:

1. A bank proof system requires both hardware and a system application that processes a bank's paper flow. Every transaction in a bank's paper work must be processed by the proof system.

2. This bank was processed by my competitor's system. The advantage was theirs, unless the application solution was inadequate. My job was to find any weaknesses and recommend a solution.

3. The first objection was overcome by pointing out that I would not give the cashier a price unless I could make a survey. My prospect reluctantly agreed to the survey. Since this order was going to cost the bank something north of $100,000 I also suspected that his bank president required a competitive proposal because of the large investment.

4. The survey uncovered many deficiencies that I documented in my proposal and executive summary.

When I met with the cashier to present my proposal, he did not want me to present my recommendation but to just give him my price. I resisted and explained that during my survey, certain weaknesses were discovered that my recommendation would correct and improve his proof requirements. He finally agreed to my presentation.

The result: I won the contract over my competitor. The total contract price was $110,000 (a very significant sale in the 1970s), some 10% higher than my competitor.

Once we successfully installed the new proof system, this cashier became a loyal user and future purchases were always won by my company.

IN SHORT:

1. Know your system or product to be able to answer questions and objections effectively.

2. Become knowledgeable enough of your systems or products so that you can answer all or most questions on the spot. You are the expert, so perform accordingly.

3. Behave diplomatically and graciously to your prospect or competitor when answering questions or objections.

4. Avoid the temptation to bad mouth your competitor during your response.

5. Concentrate on your system or product's advantage or strength.

6. Sometimes questions or objections are a good time to attempt a trial close.

WORKING A BOOTH

In some sales environments the idea of working a booth has become an objection in itself. For others, however, it is still a common practice. If you have the opportunity to work a booth, I suggest you go for it.

In my career, I attended many conventions both on a local and national basis. I never sat but stood, greeting prospects with a friendly smile and cheerful introduction. I handed each prospect an informative, small brochure that identified our products and company, along with a calling card.

NOTE: On your next trip to a convention walk around and observe people working the booths. Many of these people and their booths are not professional. They sit in their booths eating, reading newspapers, chatting among themselves and generally ignoring potential prospects passing by.

I generally worked a booth with a small staff of seasoned salespersons, capable of explaining our products, value system and company. For example, we had developed a slogan: *"Customer rated #1."* We would explain this by offering a user list that identified the many customers we served, suggesting they randomly contact anyone on the list for a testimonial. We also asked the prospect for their calling card so we could add them to our mailings. Our mailings included valuable information that could help their bank. We included information in our mailings such as business trends, regulation changes, etc. We explained to our prospects the values of our mailings.

It is important to computerize your mailings and then on a frequent basis send the promised information. Mailings can be set up by territory, produced as originals and signed by both the salesperson and your company CEO. Effective mailings are an impressive way to keep your name in front of your prospect. Consider how important name recognition is in a political campaign. The more your prospects see your name the more you will be on their minds. The next time they need your product or service, they will call.

We attended these conventions for the value they provided to our sales effort. Since most conventions in the banking world are held in places like Las Vegas and Hawaii, they were expensive so we worked hard to make the most of our opportunities.

NOTE: If you attend conventions, make it your goal to maximize the opportunity.

Consider the following:

A. *Dress appropriately*

Coordinated shirts are fashionable, but dress slacks are a must. Wear a suit and tie when appropriate.

B. *Work standing*

Save the reading, eating and visiting for your room or a restaurant. You are there to create customer interest.

C. *Be enthusiastic*

A positive, enthusiastic attitude is attractive and contagious.

D. *Be on your best game*

You won't be on your best game if you spend the evening partying. Get a good night's sleep and avoid alcohol and overeating. Even if your expense account permits, avoid excessive indulgence.

E. *Follow up*

After the convention take the prospect calling cards you collected and follow up with a simple letter of thanks and an offer of "Can we help?" or "Is there something you need help with today?" attitude.

6. *Be a professional.*

NOTE: Send an original letter in an original envelope. Sign the letter and ask your CEO or manager to also sign, as the power of your CEO's signature adds credibility to your mailing. Computer generated labels are tacky and don't look personalized.

Your face-to-face conduct is important, but so is the time when you are not in front of your prospect. Computerize their calling cards and frequently mail a personal letter reminding them of your service. Be cordial and always use a respectful, professional tone.

Early in BANKSYSTEMS corporate life, my partner and I spent some of our meager funds and attended the Minnesota Independent Bank Association's annual convention. We were not prepared, looked like amateurs and probably should have stayed home.

Our booth was comprised of a table and hand-lettered signs. Not even close to a professional image. A young man approached us and asked to speak with us. He sold portable but professional booths and offered an "I can help you" attitude. Some $3,500 later we owned a very professional booth that fit into a suitcase eligible for airfreight. We used that first booth for years, flew it to dozens of national bank conventions and presented a professional image equal to the largest companies serving the commercial bank industry.

NOTE: *Be sure to wear a nametag high on your right side. That allows your prospect to read your name as you shake hands.*

If you are invited to do conventions, think of it as a numbers game. You can play golf with a prospect and get to talk to one person. But in the massive forum of a trade show you talk to multiple prospects. Your odds of getting business increase with the number of prospects you approach — it's a no brainer.

I was once told that I should start a business teaching people how to work trade shows. Why? Because I was the most effective trade show-man he had ever seen. I stood outside the booth and talked to people. Some people think trade shows are just a waste of time but they are not. Stand outside the booth and have something that impacts your audience, a handout of what you do. Provide a list of testimonials and business success stories.

My wife, Darlene, and I were traveling to Honolulu to work the annual Independent National Bank Convention. We were seated aboard a DC10 in the middle of the plane, center seats. I was seated on the aisle and Darlene was next to me, followed by a very nice, inquisitive lady. She and my wife were visiting about various subjects, while I read a book. The plane was packed with people, probably including many bankers. After a few hours of flying, this lady interrupted my reading and began to ask me questions. Finally, she asked what I did for a living. My reply, meant to be humorous, was "I rob banks." I then went back to my reading.

The next day as I stood in front of my booth at the convention, I greeted a banker with, "Hi, my name is Daniel Holte." He smiled and replied that he knew who I was. When I asked if I had met him before, he said, "No," and went on to explain that he recognized me from the plane ride as the guy who robs banks. Oops! Since he kept a straight face and quickly departed the obvious conclusion was that he didn't think my little joke was funny. Be careful what you say in public since you never know who might overhear!

Quick Reference – Chapter 2

Overcome Objections!

→ Know your system or product – answer questions effectively.

→ Answer all or most questions on the spot.

→ Behave diplomatically and graciously to your prospect or competitor.

→ Avoid the temptation to bad mouth your competitor.

→ Concentrate on your system or product's advantage or strength.

→ Consider attempting a trial close.

Working a booth can be a worthy investment:

→Dress appropriately

→Work standing

→Be enthusiastic

→Be on your best game

→Follow up

→Be a professional

Chapter 3

Education

"Formal education will make you a living; self-education will make you a fortune." ~Jim Rohn

Everyone in sales should have a college degree. As the quote above says, a formal education will help you make a living. As we will discuss in this chapter, however, ongoing education after college and being a student of life will be the catalyst for success and increased earning potential within your career.

Why Get an Education?

A good education will benefit your business life on many levels. While it will not provide you with talent or drive (talent you are born with and drive you must foster and discipline yourself to maintain), a college degree will open doors for you. It will help you get a good job in the first place and qualify you for promotions within the company you are working for down the road. A four-year degree is the preference but there is great effectiveness in vocational training. Don't sell yourself short in education just to start making money. Somewhere down the road you may run into a roadblock for a lack of education.

My lack of a college degree held me back from promotions past district manager. When I was eligible for a regional directorship, NCR was promoting MBAs. An excellent management career and field experience didn't count enough to be given a higher opportunity.

The obvious solution is to earn a degree after high school. If you lack the opportunity for full-time attendance, take night and/or correspondence courses. Earning a degree is critical. The lack of a college degree could cost you a future promotion. It did me!

Without an education, you may end up being rejected for a position you are qualified to do because someone with less talent than you has more credentials and lands the job. It doesn't seem right, I know, especially when you possess natural talent and the drive to do a better job than someone who has three degrees and no business savvy. But oftentimes that is the way things go. Why not give yourself the most advantage within the business world and show them that you not only have the drive and talent to get the job done, but the degree after your name that makes you a highly marketable commodity.

Many of you reading this may already be working within the business world and perhaps even paying a mortgage. Perhaps you have a family at home and you don't have the luxury of devoting yourself to being a full-time student. A college degree is still attainable and it is still something you should pursue. It will come more slowly, but it may very well be the asset that will gain you a more lucrative and prestigious position down the road.

Our family doctor while my children were growing up is a great example of college later in life. He was well into his working years when he decided to go to college to pursue his dreams. He wanted to be a doctor. Imagine, going to medical school in your forties! But he did it and he became a very good and successful physician.

Another example is a young protégé of mine. He was a very skilled systems analyst, working as my technical advisor at NCR during the creation of the Minneapolis financial district. One day I asked him what he planned to do in the future. He did not possess a college degree and I convinced him to get one by going to night school. He said he was not sure, but after thinking about it, decided to attend college at night. Once completed, he began a quick advancement in the NCR Corporation. One day I received a phone call from him announcing his promotion to Vice President of NCR, a transfer to London and a new exciting opportunity for him and his family. He attributed his success to being mentored and the fact that he completed his college degree.

You don't have to go to college full-time, just get started and keep "picking away" at it until you are finished. Have you heard the cliché "Slow and steady wins the race"? It is true and it is applicable to the one who picks away at college at a manageable, steady pace. It will help you win at sales. Don't put it off — start pursing higher education now!

Some options available for obtaining a degree include night classes at a community college or online courses through a university. The University of Minnesota, for example, offers online education for a large variety of interests, including business. The courses can be taken fully online. Additionally, the Minnesota School of Business offers accredited masters, bachelors and associate degrees — all online. Distance learning has become a very useful tool for the professional. There are likely several colleges within your area that offer the same programs, but with the Internet you can attend practically any college from your home.

Now let's say you just graduated from college with a degree in Marketing, ready to conquer the world. You are fully educated and ready to apply your book learning and achieve your goal — CEO of General Motors! Your journey has just begun. Your education has just begun. You will do well to work on self-education throughout your entire career.

SELF-EDUCATION TOOLS

TOOL #1: Get to know yourself better.

Knowing your strengths and weaknesses, within your profession, is vital. If you are a poor letter writer, enroll in a creative writing course. If you are a weak speaker, join the local chapter of Toastmaster International. The point is to know what you are and are not good at and begin to work on improving on your weak areas with the tools available. Do something about your weaknesses now!

Communication skills for a person in sales are mandatory. Probably the most difficult form of communication is written. It seems that colleges must not teach creative writing as a required course, since the educated people I have worked with lack good, creative writing skills.

TOOL #2: Become a student of your business and a student of life!

Take advantage of all corporate education and seminar opportunities. When you have an opportunity to attend trade shows, take some time and visit the other exhibits. Talk to other exhibitors about their products, services, etc.

Study corporate literature, trade publications and other companies. Your goal of understanding the products you sell will always improve sales. Improved delivery results in more sales and more sales results in more money and recognition. More money and recognition result in promotions, new cars, vacations, homes, etc. You get the idea!

You can never know too much and a constant, daily habit of study will eventually help make you an expert in your field. Set aside a certain amount of time each day for study, perhaps half an hour before the start of your workday or during your lunch. The point is that knowledge is power, and it is more important to understand your company, its products, its competitors, etc., than yesterday's football scores.

In every company, information exists that we often overlook. My youngest daughter worked for a large store. She started out as a cashier, and was soon given a promotion into the Garden Center serving on the sales floor. She was very excited, since she grew up in a family that has a passion for gardening. Like many of the youngest members of a large family, she escaped much of the hands-on training her older siblings were taught. One day as she explained her new job to me, I challenged her by asking what she knew about various plants that the store sold. She answered, "What do you mean?" Once I got her attention I carefully explained that included on the little stakes poked into each pot was most of the plant's critical environmental needs. I went on to explain that during customer traffic lulls, or as she watered, she should take a few minutes and randomly read each stake with the goal to memorize the environmental needs of each plant.

If a future customer requested a plant that would do well in the shade, she then could show them a hosta. The educational value of reading simple stakes would help her serve her customers. Knowledge is power!

In your work you are surrounded by information intended to serve customers and sell products. Use this same information to improve your own knowledge level. Become a student of your business.

Read current publications, like magazines and newspapers, particularly business-worthy publications such as *Forbes, The Wall Street Journal*, etc. Read professional blogs on the internet. There is a ton of information out there that will increase your knowledge about your business.

You can also improve your knowledge by reading trade publications and the many books found online or at your public library. Develop the habit of setting aside time daily to read for vocational knowledge.

TOOL #3: Take adult community, online or college courses.

Colleges are used for obtaining a college degree, but they are also a great resource for continuing education as well and you can take classes that will improve your selling skills. Take university adult courses in areas of personal weakness. Suppose you have difficulty speaking before large groups. Take a night class in drama or public speaking. As previously mentioned, consider joining the local Toastmasters or volunteer to make a presentation at church. Practice, practice and practice until public speaking becomes as natural as talking to your mom on the telephone.

Discipline yourself to read opposing points of view and study information from a different angle. Don't be worried that you will be influenced by these opposing views. Be knowledgeable about a variety of viewpoints so that you cannot only speak about what you believe but so that you have an understanding of other views as well. This will help you understand people better. It doesn't mean you have to believe it, just understand it.

I've already shared that a personal weakness can be communication. I learned early on in my career that verbal communication is crucial in sales through a series of events, including a failed presentation I once made.

I was a newly appointed district manager of sales in Waterloo, Iowa. On an annual basis we were expected to write a business plan for the following year. My peer group, made up of other district sales managers, attended each presentation that was primarily given to our boss, the regional manager and the senior vice president of sales for NCR.

The presentations were given alphabetically by location with Waterloo being last. I had produced a reasonable report but didn't take the time to rehearse. That cost me! By the time my turn came to present my report I couldn't even speak. I choked! As I attempted to begin my voice squeaked and I stammered. The senior vice president took pity on me and asked me to sit down, explaining I had said enough. Some years later I asked the same vice president for a promotion and got turned down. Could my failed performance have had anything to do with his decision? I think so — I met my Waterloo!

A solution, had I known better back then, could have been to enroll in a public speaking course to boost my presenting confidence. At the very least, a verbal practice session in front of a live audience, like my wife, might have helped me avoid this embarrassment. Too late, the damage was done.

NOTE: Work on your weaknesses and practice, practice, practice! It will pay off with a successful performance.

QUICK REFERENCE – CHAPTER 3

Get an education:

    →Enroll in a community college or university

    →Attend night school

    →Take courses online

Use self-education tools:

    →Get to know yourself better

    →Become a student of business and of life

    →Take adult community, online or college courses

Chapter 4

Self-Discipline

"Early to bed, early to rise, makes a man healthy, wealthy and wise." ~Benjamin Franklin

It cannot be emphasized enough how vitally important good habits are. Our lives are made up of habits we do every day, from brushing our teeth, to having a cup of coffee in the morning, to the foods we eat and how we treat other people. Granted, there are always times of exception, a vacation, a crisis, like the death of a loved one, and other events that bring a temporary break in our daily habits, but for most of our lives, our habits run us.

In his poignant book, *The Greatest Salesman in the World,* Og Mandino articulates the reality that successful people have good habits and unsuccessful people have bad habits. This concept applies to every area of life: work, health, relationships, religion and education. What are your daily habits? Are there some that need to be changed, abandoned or added?

A good exercise to help you examine your daily and life habits is to take a notebook and categorize your life to include work (business), home, relationships, finances, education, fitness and religion. Under each main topic, write down your habits.

Perhaps you like what you see and feel you are succeeding in most areas of your life. Perhaps you see that you need to make some changes. What are your priorities? Do you spend more time at the gym than with your spouse? Do you log in more hours on the Internet or in front of the television than on educational endeavors? A good examination of your habits is well worth your time.

Developing a good habit that will stick takes about 90 days. That is one summer. Imagine, if you had begun fostering that good habit three months ago, it would be part of your life today. Mark my word, three months from now will be here before you know it and, if you haven't disciplined yourself to a better way, you will have wasted another opportunity to foster a good habit.

Many people think that they should start a good habit or quit a bad one and never do. Each year rolls by and only the thought remains of what "should" be done. When should we begin developing a good habit that will benefit our life and bring success? Right now! Don't start tomorrow, Monday or on New Year's Day. Start right now! Putting forth effort for a short time can help you reap a lifetime of success.

NOTE: Don't be tempted to change all your habits at once. That would be overwhelming. Take the areas of your life and identify the most destructive habit in each category and replace it with a good habit.

Perhaps you need to work on your relationships at home. A good place to start is simply how you talk to the people you live with. Choose to treat others with respect and love. You don't think they deserve it, or it isn't fair when they treat you poorly? Don't treat others based on how they treat you, but how you would like to be treated. It is the key to successful relationships.

Perhaps you need to lose some weight. Try 10 minutes of exercise a day. It doesn't seem like much, but is it more than you are doing now? Add more water into your diet, and pick fruit instead of pastries. There are many small things you can do that take little effort and time to improve your health. Resist the urge to go on a crash, get-thin-quick diet. These are a recipe for failure.

NOTE: Sure success comes with discipline and time, adding habits into your routine that you intend to keep for life.

Maybe you want to read through the Bible. It is a really, really long book and it may seem intimidating. Well, in just 10 to 15 minutes a day, the Bible can be read from cover to cover in just one year. Who doesn't have 10 minutes a day?

The point is, habits are small, daily tasks that we foster and nurture in our lives. They aren't monumental feats or get-it-done-quick schemes. They are, rather, the little things that we do each day and, if they are healthy and good, bring us success.

Speaking of business, where work is concerned, take a hard look at your habits. If you are not succeeding in this area, I suggest you make a list of habits that will bring you closer to success and prioritize them.

Don't be fooled into thinking that your personal life and your business life are separate. Who you are at home is who you are. Your personal habits will spill over into your work life. With slow and steady work, you can and will succeed in every area of life. Perfection is not the goal, healthy living in every area of life is.

FIVE BENEFICIAL AREAS OF SELF-DISCIPLINE

1. Appearance

This is very critical. It is important for professionals to resist the temptation to dress-up or dress-down. Rather, dress conservatively. No jeans or tennis shoes unless appropriate for a specific task or event like a company picnic.

Conservative wear is timeless and fits into any business situation. How you dress tells people around you if you are serious or not about business and eliminates the perception that you don't care, or that you are trying to impress others.

You can dress like a millionaire on a limited budget. If you purchase one to three conservative suits, they can be stretched to look like a larger wardrobe with a collection of shirts or blouses along with complementary accessories. Ties and scarves are inexpensive. Jewelry also adds a nice touch to an ensemble. Just make sure to avoid anything flashy — it can send the wrong message of trying too hard to impress.

Shine your shoes! Nothing is more distasteful than dull, dirty shoes. A clean professional appearance is always appropriate. And speaking of shoes, make sure they match your outfit.

I attended a conference for used equipment dealers in the early 80s, held in Sarasota, Florida. The many workshops and presentations were well organized and informative. One of the presentations was led by a very high-powered PhD in computer science. The man mounted the stage in style, dressed in a dark three-piece suit, starched white shirt and very attractive red tie. His shoes were a different story though, white tennis shoes. Hardly appropriate, and very distracting. To make matters worse, he was very animated, walking back and forth during his presentation making his appearance clownish. His white tennis shoes and animated style were enough of a distraction to render his presentation ineffective.

Your hygiene should be impeccable. Clean fingernails and conservative, well-groomed hair are both important. Subtle body scents are a must. There is nothing more distracting than a bold perfume or lotion. The opposite extreme, body odor, is just as bad, if not worse, and can spoil the professional image you are trying to maintain.

A word on body piercings and tattoos: If you must have them, keep them subtle and discrete. Avoid the temptation to display them where your clothing will not cover, even in a swimsuit. Someday you might be invited to play golf with an important client's executive and the tail of a large leopard that shows through a sports shirt will send a message. You get the idea.

When I was 16 years old I worked on a farm in southern Minnesota. I worked with a crew of older men and also spent recreation time with them. One night while attending a county fair they talked me into tattoos on each of my forearms. Years later, before tattoos became popular, I realized these tattoos were not appropriate. I had them removed by laser surgery. What cost me $25 to tattoo cost me $3,500 to remove. Fads cycle in and out of fashion, so refrain from any form of fashion or fad that provides a permanent statement.

Don't be fooled into thinking you won't be affected by the culture. What looks good today may not be in style tomorrow. A clean-cut, classic style is not dictated by trends and is always appropriate!

2. Promptness

It is critical that you present yourself as a prompt person at work. Get to work on time (15 minutes early, at least, is preferable) and resist the urge to leave before the day is done.

Deliver projects on time. A great coach once said that if you are five minutes early, you're late! It doesn't matter if everyone else, including the boss, is late. You should be early. By the way, as long as you are there early, dig in and begin working. Additionally, avoid leaving early just because you got to work before everyone else in the office.

3. Honesty

When you promise something, deliver it. Do not procrastinate and then make up some flimsy excuse for your unfulfilled commitment. That is dishonest. Honesty also means that you earn your paycheck. Do at least more than what is expected. Like I learned in the Marines, "Don't get caught backing up to the pay table." In other words, walk straight and earn your paycheck by honest means and hard work. It will earn you respect from others and even yourself!

4. Discretion

You have to be careful what you say to anybody. People have the tendency to pass on information. We all need to vent from time to time but it is wise to speak only with a trusted friend outside the workplace or a spouse. You cannot afford to be perceived as a troublemaker or someone who is negative. You have to be diplomatic enough and smart enough to avoid those conversations, even with someone who aggravates you.

Don't be a complainer. Refuse the opportunity to be negative about your company or manager. You don't have to be a prig, simply avoid complaining, or Group Company bashing.

By all means, have a sense of humor. Lighten up. It doesn't matter if you're selling or a schoolteacher, if you can't lighten up, no one will like doing business with you. Be a happy warrior.

5. Loyalty

Loyalty requires that you put forth your best effort for every assignment, even though you can't see the benefit. Loyalty also means that if you really believe any program or task is flawed, you are required to constructively offer an alternate solution. Offer your suggestion in writing to your supervisor and never go over your direct supervisor's head.

While your own appearance and habits are critical to your business life, be careful how you look at potential customers. A good salesperson never judges a prospect by his appearance. My wife and I tend to dress like bums when shopping for cars. We like to be comfortable. As our income grew, car shopping changed to luxury automobiles. Our shopping included Lincoln, Chrysler New Yorker and Cadillac.

One day, while we were car shopping, a salesperson for Lincoln ignored us based on, I am certain, our appearance. We moved on. The Chrysler people showed us mid-class and the Cadillac salesperson was just plain stupid. By the time we got to the Cadillac dealer my fuse was short. As we entered the showroom, a middle-aged salesperson approached and greeted us by asking if he could show us something used. I lost my cool, told him I could afford any priced car in the lot, gave him my calling card and left. That evening the Cadillac dealer's vice president of sales called and attempted to apologize. The salesperson must have relayed the mistake to his manager. The damage was already done. We bought the most expensive Chrysler. How do you suppose the sales manager there reacted?

As a young salesperson I observed that my manager was always demonstrating the top of his product line. When I asked why, he explained he wanted his prospect to have the opportunity to choose the best then if, for any reason, he could not justify the best a lesser solution was offered. He went on to explain that a surprising number of prospects choose the best even after considering a less expensive solution.

Quick Reference – Chapter 4

Five beneficial areas of self-discipline:

- →Appearance
- →Promptness
- →Honesty
- →Discretion
- →Loyalty

Don't judge a prospect by their appearance.

CHAPTER 5

TEAMWORK

"Individual commitment to a group effort — that is what makes a team work, a company work, a society work, a civilization work."
~Vince Lombardi

The primary art of selling is usually a solitary, individual effort. So why include a chapter on teamwork? Developing a team spirit is part of successful selling. Selling and everything else you do in life has a team approach. We all like to think "I did this on my own," but that's not true. It is always teamwork.

SEVEN ELEMENTS OF A TEAM ATTITUDE

ELEMENT #1: Be a stakeholder in your company.

I believe that everyone employed should perform as though they own their company. From the janitor to the CEO they should perform as stakeholders.

A stakeholder from the company prospective should be someone that is granted the authority to run their prospective department or division as though it was a company within a company. This means to me that these key people are given the confidence by upper management to make and manage their prospective ongoing actions without being micro-managed.

If you are a manager, when you select someone for stakeholder status you must develop a relationship of confidence. This confidence means that their performance will be judged on merit. If they are granted the authority to manage, do not be tempted to micro-manage them. Write a job description, outlining their responsibilities, read and have them sign off and then let them proceed.

Develop an open door policy. They must feel confident that they can visit over situations that are uncomfortable or outside of their authority.

If the stakeholder is micro-managed, or afraid to make decisions, you will stifle creativity or worse yet spend exorbitant amounts of time making their decisions for them. One of you isn't necessary.

How does this relate to sales? If a salesperson doesn't have the authority to complete a sale without direct authority from his or her manager, they will be crippled.

For example: A car salesperson should be given authority to complete sales within defined parameters. This is not a common practice. Training is important and guidelines are a must if a salesperson is given authority to complete sales. If tied to their commission opportunity, this will make them a stakeholder.

My wife and I recently visited an auto showroom ready to trade up to a new vehicle. We had previously visited, explained our needs to the salesperson and knew the trade value of our car, the price and discount and dealer invoice of the new car. We asked for their best price, and the salesperson could not make the deal without his sales manager getting personally involved. The salesperson didn't apparently have any authority. This person had explained to us earlier that he had sold cars for 17 years. He also shared that he had worked for this particular dealer for four years. He was very professional and seemed competent, yet he didn't have the authority to complete the sale.

The sales manager was very high-powered, didn't listen to our needs and irritated us to the point we left. Then, about a week later, he called and asked if we were ready to trade and do the deal. "No thanks, see you later," was my response.

Be a stakeholder in the company you work for and, if you are a manager, help your employees to become stakeholders.

ELEMENT #2: Ditch the "It's not my job" attitude.

When a co-worker is absent, the other staff might display an "it's not my job…" attitude. This is a poor attitude in any company, since the entire operation should be built on teamwork.

I have worked in environments where the employees assert an attitude that says they will not do any more than what is written on their job description. While it is necessary for each staff member to pull their own weight and do their jobs so that you can do yours, don't become so high and mighty in your own position that you are unwilling to answer a phone when the receptionist is away from his or her desk, or too busy to stop and pick up a piece of trash off the floor. Be a team player!

ELEMENT #3: Share information with your peers.

Sure, sharing information with your peers might help make them better individual performers, but a team spirit shared with each other might just make you all a better team.

A sales team's approach to the five steps of selling won't be equally successful. One of your sales peers will be a better proposal writer or demonstrator. Help each other improve by sharing. You will lift the entire team, improve the company and enjoy membership in a successful endeavor with the satisfaction of helping each other. Remember the old adage: A rising tide lifts all boats.

ELEMENT #4: Encourage productivity.

Promoting productivity and encouraging co-workers is a vital part of being a team player. Think about the last time someone encouraged you (I hope you can remember being encouraged) and consider how much more positive it made you feel than when you received discouragement.

It is easy to be critical of others. But it doesn't really produce success. Sometimes, constructive criticism spoken out of an attitude of helping others is beneficial, but more often encouragement will increase productivity. When you have a genuine kind word about something someone in your office did, say it. Say it right away before the moment passes. You will likely feel as encouraged as they do by just lightening up someone's mood. They will want to continue to do a good job that is recognized and you will be encouraging productivity.

Most often, actions speak louder than words and productivity, or lack of it, can be contagious. We live by a small town that includes a Dairy Queen restaurant. This spring while shopping at my favorite garden nursery on a hot day, I decided to stop for an ice cream cone. I drove through the drive-up at 3:00 p.m., the only vehicle in line, with one or two cars parked in the lot. A voice from the order station asked how she could help and I requested a small cone. "That will be $1.99, please pull up to the next window," I heard. Complying, I sat for what seemed like an eternity while the clerk on the other side of the window fussed with something. In the back some six or seven other employees leaned or milled about and visited. Finally the first clerk opened the window and greeted me, whereupon I inquired if this was a fast-food restaurant. She closed the window and said something to one of the other "leaners." After another three to four minutes the leaner sauntered over to the dispensing machine and then prepared and served my cone. My conclusion: Poor training and a lack of sense of urgency. The owner had too many clerks for the shift and even at minimum wage he was spending about $75 per hour for the so-called "fast service." The lack of productivity was contagious and it seemed as though every employee in the store had caught the disease!

ELEMENT #5: Attend meetings.

Attend meetings and team-building events within the company you represent. Not only will this help you gain a better understanding of what is going on with the people you are working with, it will show you are a team player. Some meetings are mandatory, of course, but some are optional. Attend all of the meetings you possibly can.

ELEMENT #6: Be a mentor.

When you are given the opportunity to mentor a young salesperson, the honor carries a huge responsibility. You have the opportunity to train someone and help improve their future success. You were selected to mentor because you exhibited exceptional sales and teaching skills. When mentoring, I believe you are also beginning a journey into sales management. Mentor by sharing projects. Take your protégé along during sales calls. The time spent driving between sales calls can be profitably used to teach and mentor. It might be tempting to discuss yesterday's football game, but concentrate on mentoring. The drive provides an excellent environment to mentor one-on-one without distraction.

I mentored many young salespersons during my career. Many of them went on to successful sales careers, including promotion to sales manager and corporate executive positions.

Teach your protégé to learn sales skills from you, but avoid becoming a clone. They should be encouraged to adapt your successful methods while being themselves.

My first two NCR sales managers didn't have the interest to mentor, but my third one did. His name was Jerry and he was dynamite. I soon found myself trying to be Jerry. Personality wise it didn't work, but once I learned his methods and applied my own personality my success grew. Teach this during mentoring sessions.

When mentoring someone, don't let them give you the "monkey"! Certain jobs are time consuming and difficult, such as proposal preparation. Young salespeople might be tempted to talk you into doing their proposal preparation for them. This can be called "Who's got the monkey?" They will come to you and request your assistance. Help them with advice, but don't be tempted to accept the monkey. Simply return the unfinished proposal and explain that you will review their progress when they complete the proposal. If they are hung up, give them helpful advice but don't take the monkey by doing the work yourself. What teaching value would you provide by taking the monkey? The only thing you might do is foster a lazy salesperson. You might also stifle their creativity.

When you begin to mentor someone, make sure you obligate them. Explain that your job is to give them the fundamental skills to successfully sell. Their part of the agreement is to give 100% effort. If they fail to give at least 100% you will adjust accordingly. One more commitment to teach them is to "pass it on." Explain that as they succeed and become mentors themselves they are expected to pass on what they have learned and help others as they grow in knowledge and success.

A young salesperson I hired in Waterloo, Iowa agreed to my terms as his mentor. This sales trainee's name was Dave and he had recently graduated from college. I took Dave along on all of my sales calls during his first year. I didn't realize he resented my normal habit of teaching during our drive. He shared this with an older salesperson and when I was promoted to manage Minneapolis sales, he expressed relief that he "…wouldn't have to listen to my business chatter anymore." His new manager wasn't interested in mentoring and within six months Dave confided in the same older salesperson that he missed my help. By the way, Dave went on to have a successful career in sales and within a short time was promoted to sales manager. My mentoring methods helped speed his progress.

ELEMENT #7: Have a mentor.

When I was a young salesman working for NCR a senior salesman from Minneapolis took an interest in me and mentored me in sales skills. His name was Herb and he was considered the "dean" of selling systems to commercial banks. Little did I know that years later Herb would help me in my new job as financial manager for the Minneapolis Sales District, which was organized to serve the many large banks and bank data processing center located in the Twin Cities. This new district was to be developed from Herb's territory. I had zero experience in large banks and bank data processing centers. Herb was in the twilight of his sales career and many of the technical skills required to sell high-tech data processing had passed him by. He did, however, possess invaluable connections to the people and executives he had served during his 32 years in Minneapolis.

When I was appointed the sales manager responsible for organizing the new Minneapolis district, Herb decided to retire. I implored him to stay on board long enough to once again mentor me. He agreed and helped me for two years. I didn't even know which doors to approach and without Herb's help I might have failed in my new assignment. Not only was his help invaluable, but it was fun working with my old mentor. By the way, soon after my appointment my boss suggested that since Herb was at a retirement age I should convince him to retire. My response was to convince my boss that my success depended on Herb, since I didn't even know which doors to knock on. Herb stayed.

The formative years of Minneapolis Financial required hiring and training a complete sales staff. In true form, Herb helped me mentor and teach every one of them.

Mentoring Lessons

1. Pass it on. I believe each of us has an obligation to help the "newbies" learn their sales trade.

2. Be cooperative, listen, learn and help others.

3. Condition mentoring by obligating your protégé to promise their complete devotion to the task.

4. Live up to your part of the mentoring bargain by giving your all to the effort.

5. Be available to them throughout their career. Mentoring is a life-long commitment.

6. Accept mentoring from others who are willing to contribute. Sometimes even someone younger or someone new to your company can help you. Consider what they have to say!

7. If your mentor is willing to share failure, listen. Swallow your pride and learn from the mistakes of others.

In this chapter I discussed attending meetings and team-building events as one of the elements of having a team attitude. The stories I could tell from some of the company events I have attended would fill volumes of books. One of my fondest memories, however, came during my NCR days. It is the "How I Slew the Bear" contest.

One of the sales jobs I performed within the company required quarterly regional meetings in Minneapolis where we each presented a successful sales story. These stories were called "How I Slew the Bear." Our presentations were very competitive since a $5 per member fee was required. The money was pooled and a vote was taken to determine the winner. Since there were about 60 of us, and these meetings were conducted back in the late 70s, a prize of $300 was very desirable.

One of my friends hardly ever took the time to prepare for the "How I Slew the Bear" stories, but often won the pool. He was a master at public speaking!

At one particular meeting our boss, the regional director, called on him just before lunch. I knew he called on him with only a few minutes left to get his presentation over with quickly and move on to more serious presentations.

This fellow, Gene, turned the tables on the regional manager. He got up in front of the group and carefully explained that since he worked in a rural office he didn't possess the administrative advantage the big city salespeople enjoyed. In the big city, admin would type, copy and produce overhead slides from which presentations were completed. This work, he explained, necessarily was completed by the rural salesperson him or herself. Then, with just a few minutes to lunch he gave his concluding remarks.

He held a blank 8 ½ x 11 sheet of paper in the air over his head and announced "For my first overhead…" He brought down the house and we adjourned for lunch. Later that afternoon Gene won the pool of $300.

Was that fair? Maybe not. What we can conclude, however, is that his presentation was effective and achieved his goal of winning the pool.

All of the other presentations provided useful information that helped us sell into specific customer needs. Since the presentations were presented to our peers, we could easily contact the successful salespersons for copies and advice.

Teamwork!

Quick Reference – Chapter 5

➔Be a team player:

➔Be a stakeholder of your company

➔Ditch the "It's not my job" attitude

➔Share information with your peers

➔Encourage productivity

➔Attend meetings

➔Be a mentor

➔Have a mentor

Chapter 6

Documentation

"I always say, keep a diary and someday it will keep it will keep you." ~MaeWest

Documentation is a must-do job that is made easier today by taking advantage of computer power. Why is documentation important? It provides substantial information from both successful and failed sales.

If you lose a sale, go back if possible and ask your prospect why. Be pleasant! Explain that you want to improve and enlist his or her help. You seldom will get turned down. Then listen and do not be tempted to use the meeting as another sales attempt. Be honest, listen and learn from your mistakes. Consider investing in this meeting by inviting your failed prospect to lunch. The natural lunch atmosphere will result in money well spent.

After lunch, go to your computer and document the meeting. Given the next opportunity with a similar prospect, study your failure to avoid another loss.

THREE BASIC AREAS OF DOCUMENTATION

1. File keeping of documents, including proposals, correspondences, a client list and a user list.

My style of proposal writing evolved over my sales career. I constantly refined this important document and finally produced a very effective sales tool. By the time BANKSYSTEMS was organized my proposal had been tested through many live sales and I began to realize how important and critical to my sales effort this formal documentation was. When we first organized BANKSYSTEMS I was the only employee. My business partner didn't join for the first seven months because our cash flow wasn't strong enough to even pay me.

I had saved copies of most of my sales materials generated in 20 years of selling. Documentation proved greatly beneficial to me. By the time we began to grow and add salespeople to our staff, my proposal became critical.

We were able to train inexperienced salespersons in the art of taking a survey over the phone. We used the data collected to customize proposals and many times closed a large sale, as high as $250,000, without ever traveling to the prospect's bank.

In addition to keeping proposals on file, client and user lists are also important. As I explained in the first chapter, providing a user list for potential clients is beneficial and productive. Keep your list updated and take notes on the user and client list that are not successful for your own personal reference.

Don't kid yourself that you will add new users or clients (or prospects) to your documentation later, just do it right away. One of the reasons for documentation is that relying on your memory alone is not a wise practice. Sooner or later you will forget an important piece of information.

If your files are all on the computer, don't forget to have a backup system. Your documents are a crucial part of your business.

2. Keep a diary.

Within your documentation a diary is critical. Take a few minutes after your day's activities to document important events. Your diary doesn't need to include non-important information but could be just a few notes, including:

—Names of clients and any action concluded.

—Thoughts about your perception of information you think might be critical to future contacts. An example of this might be the fact that your client's son plays hockey. On your next visit you might ask the client how "John" is doing in hockey.

—Any useful information you observe about your prospect's personal life.

This might be a good place to explain where an often-overlooked source of personal information comes from. Let's say you meet in your prospect's office. Look around, his office will tell a story from the pictures and books. Notice if the office is neat or messy. Your prospect's personal life will be on display. Be observant, it pays off.

Your prospect's habits will also be on display. Pay attention! If you are not good at reading body language, pick up a study of kinesics at your local library to help you. Your prospect's body language will provide clues to his or her personality. How can this help you become a better salesperson? By using your head! You can learn to talk with your prospect while paying attention to the way they move. If someone moves toward you, it shows they are interested. Away from or arms crossed can mean resistance. Working on the skill of reading people — also called discernment — will help you know how to better interact with your prospects and your customers.

You are computer literate, so take advantage of its usefulness. You can keep a diary on the computer and, if you like, print it out every three months or so and file it in a three-ring notebook. Place only important events, names, ideas, phone numbers, etc. in your diary. And keep it private. Avoid the temptation to share your documents or personal files with anyone else. In fact, don't even mention the diary to anyone.

A diary is a valuable reference and you never know when something you accomplished today might help you in the future. Write it down!

3. Keep a to-do file.

After I left NCR, my new job included the hiring of an administrative assistant. My assistant quickly became invaluable to me, adapting to my work style and assisting my administrative responsibility.

My assistant introduced me to an organization of my workflow called the "to-do file." This single folder contained notes, letters to be answered, meetings to attend, etc. At the end of the work day she would retrieve my file and update it with new tasks and remove completed ones. The next day she would repeat the process. Remember, this was pre-personal computers. Today, even with computers, this to-do file is useful since physical documents can be stored and acted on promptly. It also leaves your office or workspace tidy.

A. Organize a to-do file. If you don't have administrative assistance create this file on your own.

B. At the end of each workday, refresh the file, prioritize the tasks and store for the next day.

C. The to-do file will work fine with a computerized agenda since it stores all paper documents.

If Your Files are a Mess

Let's say your desk has piles and you are not sure what is at the bottom of them. Your drawers are stuffed with things that have become useless to you because new business has moved in and old business is done. How are you going to clean up the mess and create an organized workspace and organized filing system for yourself? You have basically two choices: dig in and spend all of your spare time cleaning up the mess, or begin an orderly system of today's work and pick away at yesterday's mess.

I strongly recommend choosing the latter and resisting the urge to do the monumental task of organizing all your previous work in a short period of time. Let me explain my logic: If you decide to tackle the whole mess at once, you will become overwhelmed and likely give up before the job is done. Also, you will lose track of today's work in the process. Instead, begin a daily maintenance program. Ask an office support person or a family member to help you, if necessary, and create a filing system for your current work. Each day, organize your paperwork, contacts, to-do list, etc. in an orderly fashion and maintain what you are currently working on in that manner every day. Putting something in the proper place is just as easy as putting it in a pile. Then, once you have a good, working system for current work, begin to pick away at the mess from your past business transactions.

Spend time each day properly storing and organizing your current work, then spend about 15 minutes a day (non-business hours) cleaning up your disorderly piles. This method will not only bring you closer and closer to an orderly office and work environment, but you will be developing a good system of daily documentation and filing that will bring you more success. Believe me when I say that order in your life will bring you more success. People who spend time amid chaos and waste time looking for things in piles are far less productive than those who maintain order. Isn't it your goal to be more productive, resulting in more sales and ultimately making more money during your career?

All three areas of documentation — files, diary and the critical to-do list — benefited me in my career. Writing down information and keeping old documents, neatly filed, added to my success as I worked to make sales, even while I was in management and then owner of my own company.

In an effort to drive home the value of documentation, I will share a final story. It illustrates a lesson I learned the hard way about doing my homework and this story shows exactly the sort of incident that should be documented and considered carefully in order to avoid making the same mistake in the future.

Sometimes, lack of knowledge can be embarrassing. One time I made a cold call to a rural bank in Forest City, Iowa with a trainee salesperson. We asked for a meeting with the president. A few days earlier I had called ahead and arranged the visit. We arrived about 10 minutes early and were ushered into the coffee area. A rather large gentleman was holding court, dressed like an Iowa farmer in jeans and a plaid shirt. After some 10 minutes the audience left and this man turned his attention on me. He noticed the approach book I always carried on cold calls and asked me what I did.

My proud reply was that I sold bank hardware and software that processed bank data. He then asked me if I was any good at what I did and I responded that I was the best in the business.

I then stood up and introduced myself and my trainee salesperson. "My name is John Hansen," he replied. Then I did something stupid. I asked him, "And what do you do, sir?"

His answer was, "I own this bank and also am chairman of Winnebago."

My mistake, since I didn't do my homework. I should have known the bank owner's name! This seems like a funny story, but my lack of due diligence cost me the image of professionalism. I learned another lesson: Prepare, prepare, prepare! Certain information is critical and you might drop the ball on any one of the five steps of selling without preparation. I cannot recall, but hopefully I documented the incident by writing "Research bank owners" on my to-do list!

Are the five steps in selling enough, then? For overall success, I say "no" because woven into the five steps are the other elements necessary for success presented in this book: the importance of education, a disciplined life, a team spirit and the value of documentation. Combined, these elements will lead you down a road of winning at life and winning at sales.

Quick Reference – Chapter 6

The three basics of documentation:

→Keep files of documents, including proposals, correspondences, a client list and a user list

→Keep a diary

→Keep a to-do file

If you have a mess on your hands where your filing system is concerned, organize it a little bit at a time.

A Final Note

Be a student of life and your sales career. Selling is noble work and provides the opportunity to serve others while earning an above average income.

You are going to spend a large chunk of your life working. Hopefully it will be doing something you like. When you become successful at your sales job, life will improve and your career will become easier. If you don't enjoy selling, choose something different. It's easier to work at something you like than to spend life unhappy or unfit for your job. Throughout my career I kept a personal sales territory and I used it to complete personal sales and also as a training laboratory for trainee salespeople. I literally dragged them with me on sales calls, using travel time to pound methods into their heads. This method wasn't always popular with the trainee, but very effective. It also utilized dead travel time profitably.

Once, after making a cold call to a rural bank president, on the way back to the office, I casually asked the trainee what he learned from the call. Since the prospect wasn't very talkative the trainee's response was defensive. He answered, "He hardly said anything, what do you mean?" I responded that the bank president was married, had three children, liked to sail, lived on a farm and collected tractors. How did I know all this personal information? I asked questions and studied the pictures in his office. Any information about your prospect and about his or her business is useful information. Don't think inside the box with the rest of the world, choose to see things from all angles and learn as you go!

Keep your eyes on the goal. Be willing to take prudent chances but never put your family at risk. Your family's welfare is your most important consideration. Work to your highest potential. Today, being average is considered adequate. Consider what average represents: the best of the worst and the worst of the best. In other words, average is the worst. Strive for excellence, let that be your goal and success will follow you.

The above advice comes to you from a man who adapted these principles early and stuck to the program. It worked for me and can do the same for you.

Good selling and good luck!

ABOUT THE SALESMAN ~ DANIEL HOLTE

Daniel Holte started his own business, BANKSYSTEMS, at age 49. He took a mere $2,000 in capital and created a $15 million-a-year international business working primarily with commercial banks.

Daniel grew up on a farm in Duluth, Minnesota and began working at age nine. He had a variety of jobs from collecting waste in a hospital to working in a gas station. The gas station served as early sales training. He started washing cars and was promoted to pumping gas. Daniel's boss taught him how to deal with his customers. The station was large, with 10 pumps. The gas jockeys were taught to quickly approach the customer's car, not shuffle or saunter, greet the customer and ask a single question: "Can I fill your car with premium today?" The friendly approach many times upgraded the sale from regular gas to premium. Commissions were paid for tire, battery and accessory sales. The owner of the station had a structured sales method that he taught his employees. He created a winning sales team. At one point, that station was the largest in Minnesota.

After serving in the Marines, with an honorable discharge, Daniel started selling 7UP as a route driver. There was salesmanship involved in this because the drivers were required to keep records in a route book, writing down how many cases were sold at each stop so that consecutive sales could be made. If a grocer ordered two cases, and Daniel knew he'd bought four cases the prior week and sold out, he would convince the store manager to buy at least five or six cases.

Daniel achieved acting sales manager of that company before the local bottler went bankrupt and he was laid off.

With a wife and four kids at home, Daniel took the aptitude sales test for National Cash Register (NCR) along with about 18 college graduates. With no college education, Daniel passed the test and got the job.

The key to NCR success was based on their corporate educational system. NCR had a coordinated training institute designed to incorporate on the job training with a self-motivating correspondence course. A finishing school in Dayton, Ohio, called Sugar Camp, concluded the program. Some Sugar Camp classes were compulsory, while others were voluntary. As a salesperson and later on as a manager, Daniel adopted a commitment to three weeks a year of education at Sugar Camp and required that of his salespeople.

He worked at NCR for 19 years as a student salesman, junior salesman and senior salesman. He was promoted to district manager in Waterloo, Iowa, responsible for the systems people and sales organization. He also worked a personal sales territory along with his management job. For 15 consecutive years he made or exceeded his personal sales quota. Daniel was promoted to Minneapolis District Manager Financial Major Accounts.

In 1981, he went to work for a company called Bankers/Plus in Minneapolis as their sales manager. The company financed and leased data processing systems nationally for the banking industry. When the company was sold he was promoted to executive vice president by the new owners.

After five years with Bankers/Plus, he founded BANKSYSTEMS. In his 20 years with the company, he and a business partner created three other successful businesses.

Daniel and his wife, Darlene, are retired. They raised eight children and have fourteen grandchildren and six great-grandchildren with more on the way. They live in northern Minnesota with their dog Max.

ABOUT THE CO-AUTHOR ~ DARLA SWANSON

Darla Swanson is a news editor and freelance writer. Her education and training includes journalism school, a B.A. in English from the University of Minnesota with an emphasis on creative writing and ongoing education in professional writing, proofreading and copy editing courses.

Professionally, Darla has worked in corporate writing, developing proposals for a sales department, as a freelance and staff feature writer for several newspapers, as news editor for a weekly newspaper, and has written and published online educational curriculum units and had various other freelance writing jobs.

She makes her home in northern Minnesota with her husband, two children, three dogs and a cat.

www.ingramcontent.com/pod-product-compliance
Lightning Source LLC
Chambersburg PA
CBHW071801170526
45167CB00003B/1125